THE JEWISH LAW REVIEW VOL. II

The Mishnah's Laws of Lost and Found

Bava Metzia, Chapters One and Two

by Hillel Gamoran

Illustrated by David Bleicher

Torah Aura Productions

My thanks are due to the students in the 1988-89 Adult Talmud Class at Beth Tikvah Congregation for allowing me to experiment with them in the use of this Mishnah booklet. Their questions and insights were most helpful. Special thanks go to Sheryl Cohen, Laura Lindsay, Carol Meyer and Leila Shaw who provided examples which have been incorporated into the text. I am also in debt to the Confirmation Classes of 1990 and 1991 at Beth Tikvah for trying out this text with me and to the 1990 Avoda Corps of Olin-Sang-Ruby Union Institute for engaging the material with energy and thoughtfulness.

I want to express my sincere appreciation to Madeline Russell, Lucy Swedberg and Ruth Ziegler for typing and copying the manuscript, for their patience and their attention to detail, and to Leonard Newman for providing me with the examples from Illinois State law. I also want to thank my daughter, Miriam, for her careful reading of the text and her many helpful suggestions; and my editor, Joel Grishaver, for his continuing encouragement and assistance in this project.

Most of all, my thanks are due to my wife, Judith, for her love and support. All that we accomplish in life is in partnership.

Hillel Gamoran
May 13, 1991

ISBN #978-1-934527-85-6
© 1991 Rabbi Hillel Gamoran
Illustrations © 1991 David Bleicher
Copyeditor: Lenore Bruckner

All rights reserved. No part of this publication may be reproduced or transmitted in any form or by any means graphic, electronic or mechanical, including photocopying, recording, or by any information storage and retrieval systems, without permission in writing from the publisher.
Torah Aura Productions

MANUFACTURED IN THE UNITED STATES OF AMERICA

INTRODUCTION
0.1 Judith Finds a Necklace....

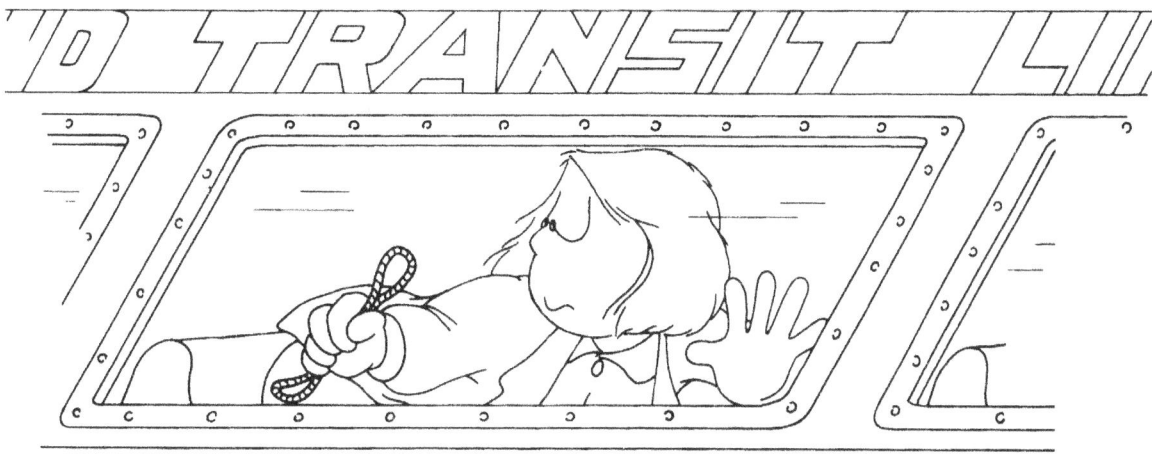

Judith took the same bus home from work every day. Usually she read the newspaper during the long ride, but today she was too tired to read. She just sat and looked out the bus window at the passing scenes.

Judith did not pay much attention to the passenger at her side. When Judith was about halfway home, her fellow passenger signaled the driver to stop, picked up several bundles and stepped off the bus.

It was then that Judith noticed, on the vacant seat beside her, a gold necklace protruding from a wrapper of tissue paper. Her fellow passenger must have been examining a newly purchased necklace and must have forgotten to replace it in her package. There lay the necklace. At first Judith wanted to call out after the woman, but the bus was already several blocks past the stop where she had alighted.

Judith was uncertain about what to do. She guessed that the necklace was worth about twenty-five dollars. Should she turn it over to the driver and ask him to put it in the lost and found office of the bus company? Should she take it to the bus company herself? Should she just leave it on the seat? Should she take it for herself? Should she bring it home and then place an ad in the newspaper? All of these questions ran through Judith's mind. The bus was approaching her stop. She had to make a decision.

Judith thought of five different courses of action. Are there any others that she might have considered? If you had been Judith, what would you have done?

The Torah Teaches About Lost and Found

The Torah, in the book of Deuteronomy (22:1-3), says that one may not ignore a lost object which is found. One must return it to its owner. Furthermore, the Torah states that if one does not know who the owner of a lost article is, one should bring it home and keep it until the owner claims it.

לֹא־תִרְאֶה אֶת־שׁוֹר אָחִיךָ	YOU SHALL NOT SEE YOUR NEIGHBOR'S OX
אוֹ אֶת־שֵׂיוֹ נִדָּחִים וְהִתְעַלַּמְתָּ מֵהֶם	OR SHEEP WANDER AWAY AND IGNORE THEM;
הָשֵׁב תְּשִׁיבֵם לְאָחִיךָ:	YOU MUST BRING THEM BACK TO YOUR NEIGHBOR.
וְאִם־לֹא קָרוֹב אָחִיךָ אֵלֶיךָ	AND IF YOUR NEIGHBOR IS NOT NEAR YOU,
וְלֹא יְדַעְתּוֹ	AND YOU DON'T KNOW WHO YOUR NEIGHBOR IS,
וַאֲסַפְתּוֹ אֶל־תּוֹךְ בֵּיתֶךָ וְהָיָה עִמְּךָ	THEN YOU MUST TAKE THE LOST ANIMAL TO YOUR HOME
עַד דְּרֹשׁ אָחִיךָ אֹתוֹ וַהֲשֵׁבֹתוֹ לוֹ:	AND CARE FOR IT UNTIL YOUR NEIGHBOR CLAIMS IT,
	AND THEN YOU SHALL GIVE IT BACK.
וְכֵן תַּעֲשֶׂה לַחֲמֹרוֹ	YOU MUST DO THE SAME FOR YOUR NEIGHBOR'S ASS,
וְכֵן תַּעֲשֶׂה לְשִׂמְלָתוֹ	OR GARMENT
וְכֵן תַּעֲשֶׂה לְכָל־אֲבֵדַת אָחִיךָ	OR ANYTHING WHICH YOUR NEIGHBOR LOSES
אֲשֶׁר־תֹּאבַד מִמֶּנּוּ וּמְצָאתָהּ	AND WHICH YOU FIND.
לֹא תוּכַל לְהִתְעַלֵּם:	YOU MAY NOT HIDE FROM THIS RESPONSIBILITY.

Deuteronomy 22:1-3

If Judith had been aware of the law of the Torah, do you think that it might have helped her decide what to do? Explain:

___

___

___

Editor's Note: The Hebrew language has no gender-free words. In Hebrew, there is no way to express laws in a gender-free manner. Thus, although the laws of the Torah and the Mishnah were written in the masculine form, they applied, in most cases, to men and women alike. The translations in this book are gender-free to reflect the idea that the laws generally applied to both sexes.

The Reason That The Mishnah Evolved

The Torah leaves unanswered many questions about lost and found articles. For example, is one required to return a small, inexpensive item, or an item whose owner cannot be identified because there are a thousand other items just like it? Also, the Torah doesn't say when to leave an article in its place because the owner may come back for it, or what to do if two people find a lost article at the same time, or what happens if an article is found on private property.

These and many more issues arose during the period after the Torah was completed. When people found lost articles and weren't sure what to do with them, or when people had other problems or disputes which they couldn't solve, they went to a *Bet Din* (a rabbinical court). Since the Bible didn't always clearly indicate to the judges of the Bet Din how to decide issues, the judges would often have to interpret the biblical law to the best of their ability and then render a decision. Over the course of the centuries, numerous rulings on many subjects were made by many judges. Finally, about the year 200 C.E., Rabbi Judah ha-Nasi, the president of the Sanhedrin (the supreme rabbinical court in Jerusalem), brought together thousands of court rulings on a wide range of subjects into a book called the *Mishnah*.

One of the parts of the Mishnah is called *Bava Metzia* (The Middle Gate). The first two chapters of Bava Metzia are a collection of laws dealing with lost and found articles. They show how the judges interpreted and expanded the law of the Torah.

If you were making a list of rules to help people decide what to do with found articles, what would that list include? Write your list on the lines below. As we read Bava Metzia, chapters one and two, you will be able to see how your list compares to that of the Mishnah.

Rules to Follow When Finding a Lost Article.

_____
_____
_____
_____
_____
_____
_____
_____
_____

UNIT I
Adam and Saul Find a Coat....

Adam and Saul were hiking in the forest when they saw a fine new woolen coat lying on the ground. They picked it up and looked at it. It had no identification on it. It looked like many other fine new woolen coats.

Whose could it be? How did it get into the middle of the forest? Adam and Saul didn't know. As they examined it, they realized that it was a better coat than either of them owned. Adam said, "Since this coat seems to have been abandoned, I think I will take it for myself." Saul looked at it and said, "I think that I would like to have it. After all, I picked it up first."

Adam retorted, "What do you mean, you picked it up first? I picked it up first."

The two men began tugging and pulling at the coat. They finally realized that if they pulled much longer, the coat would be torn and neither of them would enjoy it.

What should Adam and Saul do? Have you ever been in a similar situation? If so, what did you do? Who should get the coat?

Bava Metzia, Chapter 1, Mishnah 1

a.

שְׁנַיִם אוֹחֲזִין בְּטַלִּית,	If two people are holding a garment
זֶה אוֹמֵר אֲנִי מְצָאתִיהָ,	and one says, "I found it,"
וְזֶה אוֹמֵר אֲנִי מְצָאתִיהָ,	and the other says, "I found it,"
זֶה אוֹמֵר כֻּלָּהּ שֶׁלִּי,	or if one says, "It is all mine,"
וְזֶה אוֹמֵר כֻּלָּהּ שֶׁלִּי,	and the other says, "It is all mine,"
זֶה יִשָּׁבַע שֶׁאֵין לוֹ בָהּ פָּחוֹת מֵחֶצְיָהּ,	then one should swear to owning no less than one-half of it,
וְזֶה יִשָּׁבַע שֶׁאֵין לוֹ בָהּ פָּחוֹת מֵחֶצְיָהּ,	and the other should swear to owning no less than one-half of it,
וְיַחֲלוֹקוּ.	and they should divide it.

---

1. According to the Mishnah, who gets the coat, Adam or Saul?

2. Would the answer of the Mishnah be any different if only Adam were holding the coat when they came to court?

3. Would the court's decision be any different if there were witnesses who saw what happened when Adam and Saul found the coat?

4. Why do Adam and Saul have to take oaths? Why do they each swear that they own not less than half? Why don't they swear, as they claim, that they own it all, or why don't they swear that they own one-half?

5. Why does the court rule that they should divide it when cutting the coat in half would make it useless for both of them?

6. Suppose Adam agreed that they both picked up the coat at the same time, while Saul still maintained that he picked it up first. What then should be done?

Taking an Oath

In the Bible, and in the Talmud, taking an oath was a very serious action. It was something which Jews didn't want to do unless it was absolutely necessary. Even if people thought they were telling the truth in an oath, a mistake could cause them to swear falsely by God's name. These texts will help you understand that an oath was a very serious matter.

YOU SHALL NOT TELL A LIE USING THE NAME OF ADONAI, YOUR GOD, IN AN OATH, FOR ADONAI WILL NOT CLEAR ANYONE WHO SWEARS FALSELY BY GOD'S NAME.

Exodus 20:7 (The Ten Commandments)

IF A PERSON INTENTIONALLY GIVES FALSE EVIDENCE ABOUT A NEIGHBOR, YOU SHOULD DO TO THAT PERSON EXACTLY WHAT WAS PLANNED FOR THE NEIGHBOR. THUS YOU WILL SWEEP OUT EVIL FROM YOUR COMMUNITY—OTHERS WILL HEAR AND BE AFRAID, AND SUCH EVIL THINGS WILL NOT BE DONE AGAIN IN YOUR COMMUNITY.

Deuteronomy 19:18-20

If the court of law imposes an oath upon one of the parties, the court is permitted to bring about a settlement between them, even after the conclusion of the trial, to make sure that the one who was bound to take the oath will be exempt from the possible penalty of having taken a false oath.

Shulḥan Arukh, Ḥoshen Mishpat, Laws of Judges, 12.2

Commentary

A person taking an oath must be worthy, and there must be no suspicion of falsehood, either intentional or unintentional, in an oath. For that reason the Sages almost completely abolished oaths from court procedure and substituted other regulations. The punishment for taking a false oath is very severe since it involves the desecration of God's name.

Adin Steinsaltz, The Talmud, A Reference Guide

Bava Metzia, Chapter 1, Mishnah 1
b.

זֶה אוֹמֵר כֻּלָּהּ שֶׁלִּי	If one says (about the found garment), "All of it is mine,"
וְזֶה אוֹמֵר חֶצְיָהּ שֶׁלִּי,	and the other says, "Half of it is mine,"
הָאוֹמֵר כֻּלָּהּ שֶׁלִּי	the one who says, "All of it is mine,"
יִשָּׁבַע שֶׁאֵין לוֹ בָהּ פָּחוֹת מִשְּׁלֹשָׁה חֲלָקִים,	should swear to owning no less than three quarters,
וְהָאוֹמֵר חֶצְיָהּ שֶׁלִּי	and the one who says, "Half of it is mine,"
יִשָּׁבַע שֶׁאֵין לוֹ בָהּ פָּחוֹת מֵרְבִיעַ,	should swear to owning no less than one quarter,
זֶה נוֹטֵל שְׁלֹשָׁה חֲלָקִים	and the one should take three quarters
וְזֶה נוֹטֵל רְבִיעַ.	and the other one quarter.

---

1. This part of the Mishnah is useful in deciding a case where Adam agrees that they picked up the coat at the same time, but Saul says that he picked it up first.

    If the coat were worth $100.00, how much would Saul get? How much would Adam get?

    Saul: _____

    Adam: _____

    Do you believe that this is a fair decision? _____

    _____

Bava Metzia, Chapter 1, Mishnah 2

a.

הָיוּ שְׁנַיִם רוֹכְבִין עַל גַּבֵּי בְהֵימָה,	If two people were riding on an animal
אוֹ שֶׁהָיָה אֶחָד רוֹכֵב וְאֶחָד מַנְהִיג,	or if one was riding and the other was leading it,
זֶה אוֹמֵר כֻּלָּהּ שֶׁלִּי,	and one says, "It is all mine,"
וְזֶה אוֹמֵר כֻּלָּהּ שֶׁלִּי,	and the other says, "It is all mine,"
זֶה יִשָּׁבַע שֶׁאֵין לוֹ בָהּ פָּחוֹת מֵחֶצְיָהּ,	then one should swear to owning no less than one half of it
וְזֶה יִשָּׁבַע שֶׁאֵין לוֹ בָהּ פָּחוֹת מֵחֶצְיָהּ,	and the other should swear to owning no less than one half of it,
וְיַחֲלוֹקוּ.	and they should divide it.

b.

בִּזְמַן שֶׁהֵם מוֹדִים,	If, however, they both admit that the other has an equal claim to it,
אוֹ שֶׁיֵּשׁ לָהֶן עֵדִים,	or if they have witnesses to support their claims,
חוֹלְקִים בְּלֹא שְׁבוּעָה.	then they should divide it without taking an oath.

---

1. In what two ways is ownership of an animal demonstrated? According to the Mishnah, which way is superior?

   _____

   _____

2. Why is the oath omitted when they both admit that each has an equal claim or when witnesses testify that they have equal claims?

   _____

   _____

   _____

Additional Cases to Solve

Here are two other cases. Based on the Mishnah, what is the right thing for these people to do? Explain the reasoning behind your decision and tell why it is a just solution.

1. Manny, Moe, and Jack found nine feet of gold chain. Manny says, "We found it together." Moe says, "We found it together." Jack says, "I found it first." According to the Mishnah: (1) What does each of them need to do? (2) How much of the chain should each one get?

2. The Supercheep advertised a special compact disc player which could be ordered for half the usual price. According to the computer records, both Janet and Michael prepaid their orders on June 22. No one knows or remembers who came in first. On July 7, word came from the manufacturer that only one CD player was available and no more would be forthcoming. According to the Mishnah: (1) What does each of them need to do? (2) What happens to the CD player?

_____
_____
_____

UNIT II

Reuben is the First to See a Ten-dollar Bill—Miriam is the First to Pick It Up...

Reuben and Miriam were walking on a public sidewalk. Reuben saw something on the curb. He said to Miriam, "That looks like money over there near the grass. Please pick it up and let me see it."

Miriam walked over to it and picked it up. It was a ten-dollar bill. Miriam said, "Wow! Ten dollars! I'm going to keep it." "Just a minute," said Reuben, "I saw it first and asked you to give it to me." "Yes, but I picked it up and it belongs to me," replied Miriam.

In your opinion, who should get the ten dollars? Why?

_____

_____

_____

Bava Metzia, Chapter 1, Mishnah 3

הָיָה רוֹכֵב עַל גַּבֵּי בְהֵמָה	If someone riding on an animal
וְרָאָה אֶת־הַמְּצִיאָה,	sees something
וְאָמַר לַחֲבֵרוֹ	and says to a person standing nearby,
תְּנָה לִי;	"Give it to me,"
נְטָלָהּ וְאָמַר	and that person picks it up and says,
אֲנִי זָכִיתִי בָהּ,	"I acquired it first,"
זָכָה בָהּ.	then the person who picked it up has acquired it.
אִם מִשֶּׁנְּתָנָהּ לוֹ	But if the other gives it to the one on the animal
אָמַר אֲנִי זָכִיתִי בָהּ תְּחִלָּה,	and then says, "I acquired it first,"
לֹא אָמַר כְּלוּם.	that claim doesn't count.

---

1. According to the Mishnah, what determines ownership?

    Seeing something first _____

    Picking up something first _____

    Holding something _____

    Is this a reasonable law? Give your view and explain.

    _____

    _____

    _____

2. According to the Mishnah, who gets to keep the ten-dollar bill, Reuben or Miriam? Do you agree with the ruling of the Mishnah? Explain.

    _____

    _____

    _____

Bava Metzia, Chapter 1, Mishnah 4

a.

רָאָה אֶת־הַמְּצִיאָה,	If a person sees something on the ground
וְנָפַל עָלֶיהָ	and falls on it,
וּבָא אַחֵר וְהֶחֱזִיק בָּהּ,	and then someone else comes along and picks it up,
זֶה שֶׁהֶחֱזִיק בָּהּ	the one who has picked it up
זָכָה בָהּ.	and held it is entitled to keep it.

1. Why do you think that the person who fell on the find didn't pick it up?

   _____
   _____
   _____

Bava Metzia, Chapter 1, Mishnah 4
b.

רָאָה אוֹתָן רָצִין אַחַר מְצִיאָה,	If an owner saw people running after a find in his/her field *for example,*
אַחַר צְבִי שָׁבוּר,	after a lame deer,
אַחַר גּוֹזָלוֹת שֶׁלֹּא פָרְחוּ,	or after pigeons that could not fly,
וְאָמַר זָכְתָה לִי שָׂדִי,	and the owner said, "They are mine because they are in my field,"
זָכְתָה לוֹ.	then they are the owner's.
הָיָה צְבִי רָץ כְּדַרְכּוֹ	But if the deer could run in the normal manner
אוֹ שֶׁהָיוּ גּוֹזָלוֹת מַפְרִיחִין,	or if the pigeons could fly,
וְאָמַר זָכְתָה לִי שָׂדִי,	and the owner said, "They are mine because they are in my field,"
לֹא אָמַר כְּלוּם.	then the owner's claim doesn't count.

---

1. Why should the owner of a field be granted ownership of a find?

   _____

   Why is it right that the owner of a field be entitled to the find rather than the person who saw the find first?

   _____

   _____

2. What difference does it make if the deer is lame or if the pigeons can't fly?

   _____

3. Do you agree with the ruling of the Mishnah?

   _____

4. Laura and her sister, Irene, spend their summers at their parents' lakeside cabin in Wisconsin. The property includes several acres of wooded land behind the cabin. Laura and Irene love to go for walks in the wooded area. They know that at certain times people come to the area to hunt for rabbits, ducks and other small animals. This bothers the girls very much. One day they heard some gunshots close by. They were startled to see a beautiful gray rabbit moving very slowly. It was bleeding. Then they saw some men striding toward the rabbit. Laura and Irene screamed for the men to go away. They cried, "You have no right to be here. The rabbit is ours." They wanted to take the rabbit into the house and help it get better. The hunters, however, claimed that the rabbit was theirs and showed their hunting permits.

Who should get the rabbit?

___

Can the Mishnah help in deciding this case?

___
___
___

Unit III

Joel, Age 5, Finds a Valuable Coin, and His Father Takes Possession Of It...

Joel, age 5, was digging in the sand at the public beach. While making a particularly deep hole he discovered an 1847 American gold coin. Joel showed his find to his father. Joel's father showed the coin to a dealer who offered him $150 for it. Joel, however, didn't want to sell it. He wanted to keep the coin because it was pretty and because he was proud of himself for having found it. But Joel's father said that he needed to sell the coin. The $150 would help him to meet the heavy family household expenses.

In your opinion, who should get the coin, Joel or his father?

_____

Give your reasons.

_____

_____

_____

Bava Metzia, Chapter 1, Mishnah 5

a.

מְצִיאַת	An object found by a man's*
בְּנוֹ	minor son
וּבִתּוֹ הַקְּטַנִּים,	or daughter
מְצִיאַת עַבְדּוֹ וְשִׁפְחָתוֹ הַכְּנַעֲנִים,	or by his Canaanite slave
מְצִיאַת אִשְׁתּוֹ	or by his wife
הֲרֵי אֵלּוּ שֶׁלּוֹ	belongs to him.

b

מְצִיאַת	An object found by someone's
בְּנוֹ וּבִתּוֹ הַגְּדוֹלִים,	adult children
מְצִיאַת עַבְדּוֹ וְשִׁפְחָתוֹ הָעִבְרִים,	or by his Hebrew slave
מְצִיאַת אִשְׁתּוֹ שֶׁגֵּרְשָׁהּ	or by his divorced wife,
אַף עַל פִּי שֶׁלֹּא נָתַן כְּתֻבָּתָהּ,	even if he has not yet paid the divorce settlement,
הֲרֵי אֵלּוּ שֶׁלָּהֶן.	belongs to them.

*This mishnah clearly applied to men and thus has not been translated gender neutral.

To understand this mishnah we need to consider the position of children, slaves and wives in Mishnaic times.

Children

Fathers were responsible for the welfare of their children. A father had to provide for the food, clothing and shelter of his minor children. He was also responsible for their education. He was also liable for their misdeeds. That meant that if they damaged someone's property, he often had to pay for the damage.

Some authorities taught that a father's responsibility lasted until a daughter became 12 year of age and a son, 13. Others established different rules for determining the point at which a child ceased to be a minor.

Slaves

The Bible has separate laws for Hebrew slaves and for Canaanite slaves.

> "IF YOU BUY A HEBREW SLAVE,
> THE SLAVE SHALL SERVE YOU FOR SIX YEARS
> AND THEN GO FREE IN THE SEVENTH YEAR WITHOUT PAYMENT."
>
> Exodus 21:2

> "THE CHILDREN OF THE STRANGERS WHO LIVE AMONG YOU...
> YOU MAY BUY THEM AS POSSESSIONS.
> AND YOU MAY MAKE THEM AN INHERITANCE FOR YOUR CHILDREN AFTER YOU
> TO HOLD AS PROPERTY;
> YOU MAY KEEP THEM AS YOUR SLAVES FOREVER."
>
> Leviticus 25:45-46

A Hebrew became a slave by selling himself to pay for a debt or, in the case of a thief, when the court sold him into slavery to pay for what he stole. In either case, his period of slavery (with certain exceptions) was for six years.

Canaanite, or non-Jewish, slaves were acquired by purchase. A Canaanite slave served his master for life.

A slave owner was required to provide for his slave's needs. Strict laws existed to prevent an owner from mistreating his slave.

Wives

A husband was required to maintain his wife and provide for her needs. She was allowed to retain ownership of whatever property she possessed before the marriage, but, during the marriage, he controlled that property and, if it produced income, he received it. If he died or divorced her, the property remained hers. While married, any property the wife acquired or any income she earned were controlled by her husband.

1. According to the Mishnah, is Joel's father allowed to sell the coin and use the proceeds for family expenses? May he use the money for his own personal pleasure? How old would Joel have to be to be allowed to keep the coin?

   _____
   _____
   _____
   _____

2. Do you agree with the Mishnah? Explain your view.

   _____
   _____
   _____
   _____

3. Why did the Mishnah make a distinction between a Canaanite slave and a Hebrew slave?

   _____
   _____
   _____
   _____

4. Why did the Mishnah rule that a wife's find belonged to her husband? In what way was it fair? In what way was it unfair? Would it be fair today?

   _____
   _____
   _____
   _____

UNIT IV

Marla Finds Legal Documents....

Marla was the last one to leave the courthouse. As she walked down the corridor she saw a brown briefcase on a bench. She wondered who might have forgotten it. There were no name or initials on the briefcase. When she looked inside, most of the documents dealt with a lawsuit between a Mr. Brown and a Mr. Green. The papers looked important. The person who lost them might need them before the next morning. She wanted to return them right away, but she didn't know whether they belonged to someone representing Mr. Brown or someone representing Mr. Green. What do you think Marla should do?

Bava Metzia, Chapter 1, Mishnah 7

מָצָא	If a person found
גִּטֵּי נָשִׁים,	bills of divorce,
וְשִׁחְרוּרֵי עֲבָדִים,	or deeds of freedom for slaves,
דְּיָתֵיקִי,	or wills,
מַתָּנָה,	or notes bestowing gifts,
וְשׁוֹבְרִים,	or receipts for payments made,
הֲרֵי זֶה לֹא יַחֲזִיר,	the person should not return them to the one who would benefit from them,
שֶׁאֲנִי אוֹמֵר כְּתוּבִים הָיוּ וְנִמְלַךְ עֲלֵיהֶם שֶׁלֹּא לִתְּנָם.	for the one who wrote them may have had a change of heart and decided not to deliver them.

Bava Metzia, Chapter 1, Mishnah 8

a.

מָצָא אִגְּרוֹת...	If a person found documents…
וְכָל מַעֲשֵׂה בֵית דִּין,	executed by a court of law,
הֲרֵי זֶה יַחֲזִיר.	the person should return them to the one who would benefit from them.

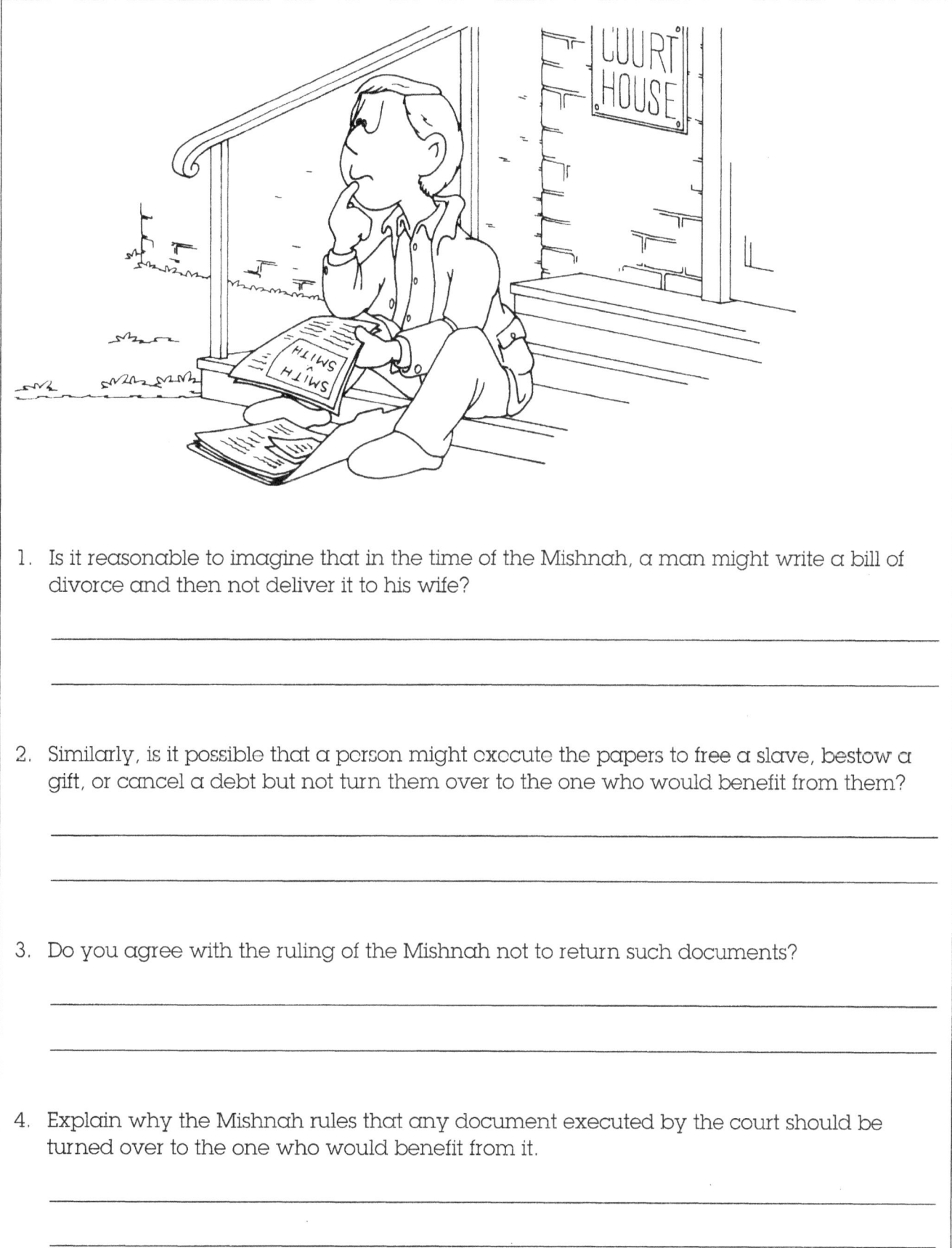

1. Is it reasonable to imagine that in the time of the Mishnah, a man might write a bill of divorce and then not deliver it to his wife?

   _____
   _____

2. Similarly, is it possible that a person might execute the papers to free a slave, bestow a gift, or cancel a debt but not turn them over to the one who would benefit from them?

   _____
   _____

3. Do you agree with the ruling of the Mishnah not to return such documents?

   _____
   _____

4. Explain why the Mishnah rules that any document executed by the court should be turned over to the one who would benefit from it.

   _____
   _____

Bava Metzia, Chapter 1, Mishnah 8 b.

מָצָא	A person who finds
בַּחֲפִיסָה,	a document in a leather pouch
אוֹ בִּדְלוּסְקְמָא,	or in a case,
תַּכְרִיךְ שֶׁל שְׁטָרוֹת	a roll of documents
אוֹ אֲגוּדָּה שֶׁל שְׁטָרוֹת,	or a bundle of documents,
הֲרֵי זֶה יַחֲזִיר.	should return them.
וְכַמָּה אֲגוּדָּה שֶׁל שְׁטָרוֹת?	**Q:** And how many make a bundle of documents?
שְׁלֹשָׁה קְשׁוּרִין זֶה בָזֶה.	**A:** Three tied together.

c.

רַבָּן שִׁמְעוֹן בֶּן גַּמְלִיאֵל אוֹמֵר,	Rabbi Simon ben Gamliel says:
	If the documents deal
אֶחָד הַלֹּוֶה מִשְּׁלֹשָׁה	with one borrower from three lenders,
יַחֲזִיר לַלֹּוֶה;	one should return them to the borrower.
	If they deal
שְׁלֹשָׁה הַלֹּוִין מֵאֶחָד	with three borrowers from one lender,
יַחֲזִיר לַמַּלְוֶה.	one should return them to the lender.

---

1. How does the Mishnah help Marla to make a decision?
   _____

2. Why does the Mishnah rule that a bundle of documents should be returned?
   _____

3. Do you agree that a bundle of documents consists of at least three?
   _____

4. What is the logic behind Rabbi Simon ben Gamliel's ruling? Do you agree with it?
   _____

REVIEW
Who Gets It?

The class is divided into four groups. Let each group dramatize one of the first four examples in this exercise.

1. Orly saw a stray dog running on Becky's front lawn. As it ran across the street, Orly caught it and took it home. Becky objected. Since it was observed on her lawn, she felt that it should belong to her.

2. Janet was separated but not yet divorced from Herman. When Janet found a twenty-dollar bill on the street, Herman said that she should give it to him to help him pay the doctor bills for their sick child. Janet said that she needed it for her own personal use.

3. Marc and Justin each lent their footballs to boys on the block. At the end of the season only one boy, Don, admitted to borrowing a ball, but he didn't remember whether it was Marc's or Justin's. Marc was sure that he had lent the ball to Don. Justin was equally sure that he was the lender.

4. Pauline and Jennie were in the parking lot of the supermarket. Pauline was in the car. Jennie was standing nearby. Pauline saw a loose dollar on the ground. She asked Jennie to pick it up for her. Jennie picked it up and gave it to Pauline who thanked her and was delighted to have an extra dollar.

   Then Jennie decided that the dollar belonged to her, since she had picked it up.

5. Jerry found an IOU on the street. It said that Henry Bartlett owed George Bates one hundred dollars.

_____

_____

6. Stephanie found a brown envelope in the park. In it were three IOUS. Each IOU was for fifty dollars. Each one stated that John Peterson was the lender. The borrowers were Robert Elson, Paula Temple and Jeffrey Watson.

_____

_____

The Mishnah Teaches

Write True or False next to each statement. Where the statement is true according to the Mishnah, tell whether or not you agree with this teaching of the Mishnah and give your reasons. Where the statement is false according to the Mishnah, correct it and then comment.

_____ 1. Possession indicates ownership.

_____

_____ 2. Whatever crosses someone's field belongs to the owner of the field.

_____

_____ 3. The best way to show ownership of an animal is to ride it.

_____

_____ 4. Lost documents should be returned to whomever wrote them.

_____

_____ 5. The find of a financially independent person belongs to the finder. The find of someone who is financially dependent on someone else belongs to the person who is supporting the finder.

_____

Brain Teasers

1. Marlon tends pigeons on the roof of his apartment building. There is a parapet (a low wall around the roof). One day, when he is racing his pigeons, a stray pigeon, with a broken wing, lands on the roof and is unable to take off again. Marlon says, "This pigeon is now mine." At the same time, Jackie (his next door neighbor), says, "I want the pigeon." They go over to the bird and both touch it at the same time. On the bird's leg they find a message capsule. When they open it up they find a message which says: "The Don will pay Guido $2,500 when the job is complete." According to the Mishnah, what should be done with the message?

_____
_____
_____

2. Jeff is Hank's stepson. Hank married Jeff's mother and has adopted both Jeff and his sister Marge. One day, Jeff broke a window with a foul ball that went really long. Hank chased Jeff into the woods where the two of them found an abandoned pony with a note which said, "Whoever finds this pony may keep it." When they came out of the woods, Jeff was riding the pony and Hank was leading it. Each of them claimed, "I found it first!" According to the Mishnah: (1) What does each of them need to do? (2) What should happen to the abandoned pony?

_____
_____
_____

3. In a football game, Darrell kicks off and Ralph catches the ball. When the ball is in Ralph's hands, he says, "The ball is mine." Jon tackles Ralph, and the ball is fumbled. Fred shouts to Beaver, "Get the ball for me." Meanwhile, Beaver picks it up and says, "The ball is mine." Susan grabs the ball, and says, "No, the ball is mine." Meanwhile, Charles takes a flying dive for the ball, misses, and finds a file folder sitting by the side of the road. In it are a set of discipline letters written by Mr. Grishaver, intended to be sent home to the parents of David, David, Davida, Brett, Shane, Shane, Kent, Erika, Jason, Danny, Ben, Erin, B.J. and Andy to be signed and returned. There are no parent signatures on the documents. According to the Mishnah, what should Charles do?

_____

_____

_____

UNIT V

Karen Finds a Scarf

Marshall Field's was in the middle of its annual sale. The store was very crowded, and shopping took a long time. But Karen was glad that she had gone. She bought several items which she really needed.

She made her way out to the parking lot with her arms full of bundles. As she was about to get into her car, she saw a Marshall Field's bag on the ground. It was just like the bags she was carrying. She put her packages inside her car and then picked up the bag from the ground. Inside was a beautiful scarf. There was also a sales slip. It said "Marshall Field's, $119.00 cash, paid."

Karen looked at the scarf. It was not unique. There were hundreds like it, but she liked it very much. She put it in her car and took it home with the rest of her bundles.

Did Karen do the right thing? Should she have returned it to Marshall Field's? Explain your point of view.

_____
_____
_____
_____

Bava Metzia, Chapter 2, Mishnah 1

a.

אֵלּוּ מְצִיאוֹת שֶׁלּוֹ	A person may keep some finds,
וְאֵלּוּ חַיָּב לְהַכְרִיז.	but others must be proclaimed.
אֵלּוּ מְצִיאוֹת שֶׁלּוֹ,	The following finds may be kept:
מָצָא פֵּירוֹת מְפֻזָּרִין,	scattered fruit,
מָעוֹת מְפֻזָּרוֹת,	scattered money,
כְּרִיכוֹת בִּרְשׁוּת הָרַבִּים	small sheaves of grain in the public domain,
וְעִגּוּלֵי דְבֵילָה,	cakes of figs,
כִּכָּרוֹת שֶׁל נַחְתּוֹם,	loaves of bakers' bread,
מַחֲרוֹזוֹת שֶׁל דָּגִים,	strings of fish,
וַחֲתִיכוֹת שֶׁל בָּשָׂר,	pieces of meat,
וְגִזֵּי צֶמֶר	wool shearings
הַבָּאוֹת מִמְּדִינָתָן,	as they come from their place of origin,
וַאֲנִיצֵי פִשְׁתָּן	bundles of flax
וּלְשׁוֹנוֹת שֶׁל אַרְגָּמָן,	or strips of purple wool,
הֲרֵי אֵלּוּ שֶׁלּוֹ.	these belong to the finder.
דִּבְרֵי רַבִּי מֵאִיר.	This is the view of Rabbi Meir.

b.

רַבִּי יְהוּדָה אוֹמֵר,	Rabbi Judah says:
כָּל־שֶׁיֵּשׁ בּוֹ שִׁנּוּי	"Everything that contains something unusual
חַיָּב לְהַכְרִיז.	must be proclaimed.
כֵּיצַד?	For example,
מָצָא עִיגוּל וּבְתוֹכוֹ חֶרֶס,	if someone finds a cake with a potsherd inside it
כִּכָּר וּבְתוֹכוֹ מָעוֹת.	or a loaf of bread with a coin inside it."

c.

רַבִּי שִׁמְעוֹן בֶּן אֶלְעָזָר אוֹמֵר,	Rabbi Simon ben Elazar says:
כָּל־כְּלֵי אַנְפּוֹרְיָא אֵין חַיָּב לְהַכְרִיז.	"All new merchandise need not be proclaimed."

1. Can the Mishnah help Karen decide what to do with the scarf? Give your view.

   _____

   _____

2. Are the opinions of Rabbi Meir, Rabbi Judah and Rabbi Simon contradictory or complementary? Explain.

   _____

   _____

   _____

3. How does one proclaim a find today?

   _____

   _____

   _____

Bava Metzia, Chapter 2, Mishnah 2

וְאֵלּוּ חַיָּב לְהַכְרִיז	The following finds, one must proclaim:
מָצָא פֵירוֹת בִּכְלִי	fruit in a container
אוֹ כְּלִי כְּמוֹת שֶׁהוּא,	or an empty container,
מָעוֹת בְּכִיס	money in a purse
אוֹ כִּיס כְּמוֹת שֶׁהוּא,	or an empty purse,
צִבּוּרֵי פֵירוֹת,	a pile of fruit,
צִבּוּרֵי מָעוֹת,	a pile of money,
שְׁלֹשָׁה מַטְבְּעוֹת זֶה עַל גַּב זֶה,	three coins on top of each other,
כְּרִיכוֹת בִּרְשׁוּת הַיָּחִיד	small sheaves *of grain* on private property,
וְכִכָּרוֹת שֶׁל בַּעַל הַבַּיִת,	homemade loaves of bread,
וְגִזֵּי צֶמֶר	wool shearing
הַלְּקוּחוֹת מִבֵּית הָאֻמָּן,	which come from the craftsman's shop,
כַּדֵּי יַיִן, וְכַדֵּי שֶׁמֶן,	jars of wine or jars of oil,
הֲרֵי אֵלּוּ חַיָּב לְהַכְרִיז.	these must be proclaimed.

1. Apply the Mishnah to each item below were it found on a crowded street in a large city, indicating whether it could be kept by the finder or whether it had to be advertised.

A one-dollar bill.	Keep	Advertise
A fifty-dollar bill.	Keep	Advertise
Three five-dollar bills on top of each other.	Keep	Advertise
A wallet containing fifty dollars but with no I.D.	Keep	Advertise
A new white sweater.	Keep	Advertise
A Palatine High School jacket.	Keep	Advertise
A used Minolta camera.	Keep	Advertise
A brown dog with white spots.	Keep	Advertise

2. Daniel was a summer resident at a popular campground in Wisconsin. Some of the residents, like Daniel, stayed for the whole summer, but there were also many who came only for a short time. One day, when Daniel visited the public rest room, he saw a gold wedding ring on the shelf above the sink. What should Daniel do about the ring?

   _____

   _____

3. As Jayne was walking into the supermarket to do her weekly grocery shopping, she saw a small piece of folded paper. She picked it up and realized that it was a fifty-dollar bill folded into a small square. What should she do?

   _____

   _____

4. The law of the State of Illinois (amended January 1, 1984) says that if a person finds lost goods or money, he must inform the owner, if known, and must return what was lost without compensation, except such compensation as is voluntarily given by the owner.

   Do you agree that a person should be required by law to return a find to its owner without any compensation? Explain.

   _____

5. The Illinois statute further states that if the owner is unknown, the finder must advertise the find. Do you feel that this is an appropriate law? Explain your viewpoint.

   _____

   _____

6. What is the law in your state? Does it differ from the Illinois law? In what ways? In your opinion, is it a better law than that of the State of Illinois?

   _____

   _____

UNIT VI
Murray Finds a Coin in Helen's Chair

Murray came to visit his friend Helen. He sat down on her most comfortable lounge chair, which she had owned for ten years. While relaxing, he absentmindedly put his hand below the cushion. He felt a coin. He pulled it out and noticed that it was an Eisenhower silver dollar, now worth more than five dollars. He felt fortunate to discover such a find since he was somewhat short of cash. But when he showed it to Helen, she said that it belonged to her since he had found it in her chair in her house.

Who gets the silver dollar? Defend your view.

_____

_____

_____

_____

Bava Metzia, Chapter 2, Mishnah 3

a.

מָצָא	If someone finds
אַחַר הַגָּפָה	behind a fence
אוֹ אַחַר הַגָּדֵר	or behind a hedge
גּוֹזָלוֹת מְקֻשָּׁרִין	pigeons tied together
אוֹ בִּשְׁבִילִין שֶׁבַּשָּׂדוֹת,	or on paths in the fields,
הֲרֵי זֶה לֹא יִגַּע בָּהֶן.	they should not be touched.
מָצָא כְּלִי בָּאַשְׁפָּה,	If someone finds an article on a junk heap,
אִם מְכֻסֶּה לֹא יִגַּע בּוֹ,	—if it is covered, it should not be touched;
אִם מְגֻלֶּה נוֹטֵל וּמַכְרִיז.	—if it is uncovered, it should be taken and proclaimed.

b

מָצָא בְגַל	If someone finds something in a pile of rubble
אוֹ בְּכֹתֶל יָשָׁן	or in an old wall,
הֲרֵי אֵלּוּ שֶׁלּוֹ;	it belongs to the finder;
מָצָא בְּכֹתֶל חָדָשׁ,	if someone finds something in a new wall
מֵחֶצְיוֹ וְלַחוּץ	if it was on the outside of the wall,
שֶׁלּוֹ,	it belongs to the finder,
מֵחֶצְיוֹ וְלִפְנִים	but if it was on the inside,
שֶׁל בַּעַל הַבַּיִת.	it belongs to the owner of the house.

c.

אִם הָיָה מַשְׂכִּירוֹ לַאֲחֵרִים,	If, however, the house is rented to others,
אֲפִלּוּ בְּתוֹךְ הַבַּיִת,	then even if it is found inside the house,
הֲרֵי אֵלּוּ שֶׁלּוֹ.	it belongs to the finder.

1. Does the Mishnah help in deciding whether the coin belongs to Murray or Helen? Explain.

    _____

    _____

2. Would the answer based on the Mishnah be any different if Murray had found the coin in the chair of a hotel lobby? Explain your answer. Do you agree with the Mishnah?

    _____

    _____

3. Why does the Mishnah specify that birds found tied together and in out-of-the-way places should be left alone? Would it make a difference if they were found on a public thoroughfare?

    _____

    _____

4. What difference does it make whether a utensil found on a junk heap is covered or uncovered? Can you explain the reasoning of the Mishnah? Do you agree with it?

    _____

    _____

5. Why does it make a difference whether a find is discovered on the inside or the outside of a wall?

    _____

    _____

6. Harry was the last one to leave the Temple after a Sunday afternoon event. As he was walking down the steps he noticed something among the bushes. He looked more carefully. There were four books tied together with string and covered with a plastic bag. They were almost completely hidden from the sidewalk. What should he do?

    _____

    _____

UNIT VII
Bava Metzia, Chapter 2, Mishnah 4

a.

מָצָא בַּחֲנוּת	If a person finds something in a store,
הֲרֵי אֵלּוּ שֶׁלּוֹ;	it belongs to the finder,
בֵּין הַתֵּיבָה	but if it were found between the counter
וְלַחֶנְוָנִי	and the place where the storekeeper stands,
שֶׁל חֶנְוָנִי;	it belongs to the storekeeper;

b.

לִפְנֵי שׁוּלְחָנִי	If a person finds money in front of the stool of a moneychanger
הֲרֵי אֵלּוּ שֶׁלּוֹ;	it belongs to the finder,
בֵּין הַכִּסֵּא	but if it were found between the stool
וְלַשׁוּלְחָנִי	and the place where the moneychanger stands,
הֲרֵי אֵלּוּ שֶׁל שׁוּלְחָנִי.	it belongs to the moneychanger.

c.

הַלּוֹקֵחַ פֵּירוֹת מֵחֲבֵרוֹ	If someone buys produce from a neighbor
אוֹ שֶׁשָּׁלַח לוֹ חֲבֵרוֹ פֵּירוֹת	or if a neighbor sends produce to someone
וּמָצָא בָּהֶן מָעוֹת	and money is found with the produce,
הֲרֵי אֵלּוּ שֶׁלּוֹ.	the money belongs to the finder,
אִם הָיוּ צְרוּרִין	but if the money was tied together,
נוֹטֵל וּמַכְרִיז.	the finder must take it and proclaim it.

1. Why does it matter whether the find is discovered in front of the counter or behind the counter?

2. If a person were to buy a bag of oranges at the grocery store and find a five-dollar bill in the bag, it wouldn't seem right to keep the money. To follow the principle of returning lost objects to their owner, it would seem that he should return the money to the grocer. Why then does this Mishnah say that if someone finds money with the produce he has bought, he may keep it? What must have been the circumstances of the sale which caused the Mishnah to rule in this way?

3. Do you agree with the Mishnah?

4. What should be done with a twenty-dollar bill found on the street in front of the American National Bank?

   on the ground in front of the bank? _____

   on the floor of the bank lobby? _____

   in the office of the president of the bank in front of the president's desk? _____

   behind the president's desk? _____

5. What should be done if one finds ten one-dollar bills with a band around them on a counter in the bank?

6. Shauna had a very hard day at the office. She was very tired, but after work she had a few errands to do. She spent $17.41 at the supermarket, $8.99 at the drug store, and $5.50 at the dry cleaners. She didn't bother to count her change at any of these places; she simply stuffed the change into her wallet. She knew that she had started the day with only a fifty-dollar bill in her wallet. In the evening, she went through her wallet. She had a twenty-dollar bill, a five-dollar bill, three singles and a dime. What should Shauna do?

The class is divided into pairs. Each pair makes up and dramatizes a case in which scrupulous honesty is discussed (e.g. getting something without paying for it, returning something given to you in error, cheating an insurance company, the telephone company, the government, an airline). The students give their opinions about each case.

This Mishnah is different from the others we have studied. It isn't really designed to teach a new law. Rather, it states two general principles (*K'lalim*) about the rules we have already learned. In order to understand it, we need to reread this biblical text.

> YOU SHALL NOT SEE YOUR NEIGHBOR'S OX
> OR SHEEP WANDER AWAY AND IGNORE THEM;
> YOU MUST BRING THEM BACK TO YOUR NEIGHBOR.
>
> AND IF YOUR NEIGHBOR IS NOT NEAR YOU,
> AND YOU DON'T KNOW WHO YOUR NEIGHBOR IS,
> THEN YOU MUST TAKE THE LOST ANIMAL TO YOUR HOME
> AND CARE FOR IT UNTIL YOUR NEIGHBOR CLAIMS IT,
> AND THEN YOU SHALL GIVE IT BACK.
>
> YOU MUST DO THE SAME FOR YOUR NEIGHBOR'S ASS OR GARMENT
> OR ANYTHING WHICH YOUR NEIGHBOR LOSES AND WHICH YOU FIND.
>
> YOU MAY NOT HIDE FROM THIS RESPONSIBILITY.
>
> Deuteronomy 22:1-3

Bava Metzia, Chapter 2, Mishnah 5

Q: When it says in the Torah (Deuteronomy 22:3)
that every lost object must be returned,
the garment was included.

אַף הַשִּׂמְלָה הָיְתָה בִּכְלַל כָּל־אֵלֶּה,

Why then was it explicitly mentioned?

לָמָּה יָצָאת?

A: In order to compare it to other lost articles,

לְהַקִּישׁ אֵלֶיהָ

to show that:

לוֹמַר לָךְ,

    just as a garment is distinguished by having identifying signs

מַה־שִּׂמְלָה מְיוּחֶדֶת שֶׁיֵּשׁ בָּהּ סִימָנִים

    and by having people who will want to claim it,

וְיֵשׁ לָהּ תּוֹבְעִים,

    so any lost object which has

אַף כָּל־דָּבָר שֶׁיֵּשׁ בּוֹ

        identifying signs

סִימָנִים

    and people who will want to claim it

וְיֵשׁ לוֹ תּוֹבְעִים

must be proclaimed.

חַיָּב לְהַכְרִיז.

1. Why did the rabbis use a found garment as the center of the dispute in the first case in Bava Metzia? (Remember: "If two people are holding a garment and one says, 'I found it...'')

   _____

2. According to this Mishnah what are the two basic common principles to responding to any found object?

   _____

What should you do if you find one of the following lost objects?

Write K or A in the proper column to indicate whether the item may be kept or should be advertised.

		According to Your opinion	The Mishnah
1.	New raincoat		
2.	Old baseball glove		
3.	New Cubs cap		
4.	Class ring		
5.	Kennedy half-dollar		
6.	Can of Diet Coke		
7.	Webster's Collegiate Dictionary in fairly good condition		
8.	Omega watch, looks like new		
9.	Disneyland T-shirt, very pretty but very common		
10.	Purse with $35.00 in it		

Challenge Case:

Fred, Barnie, and Melanie ditch sixth period. They head to the local supermarket in order to get a snack.

_____ Outside the store they find an unopened box of cookies lying on the wall around the parking lot. They touch it together and say, "Ours."

_____ Then, on the rack under a shopping cart left in a parking space they find a shopping bag full of potato chips, candy, and other junk food.

_____ They go into the store and start shopping. In the second aisle, lying on the floor they find a five-dollar bill. Fred and Barnie grab it together and say, "It's mine."

_____ In the fourth aisle, they find an envelope with $17.23 in it. There is no return address or notification on it. Melanie grabs it and says, "I found it—this one is mine." At virtually the same time, Fred grabs at it and says, "We found it together, it is ours."

_____ In the paper goods aisle, a watermelon is sitting on the floor. Fred picks it up and says, "This is mine."

_____ In the drinks section, Barnie picks up a six-pack of soda and finds a ten-dollar bill stuck in the plastic ring.

Note the Mishnah numbers and the answer alongside each item.

UNIT VIII

Michelle and Susan Make an "Old" Find...

It is March. Susan and Michelle go to the beach. While they are climbing along some of the rocks and cliffs, they find a knapsack filled with 50 tubes of suntan lotion. Based on the amount of dirt and stains on the knapsack, it may well have been sitting out on the rocks since last summer. What should they do?

_____

_____

This case introduces a new category in our investigation of found objects. What is that category?

_____

_____

Bava Metzia, Chapter 2, Mishnah 6

a.

וְעַד מָתַי חַיָּיב לְהַכְרִיז?	For how long a period is a person required to advertise a find?
עַד כְּדֵי שֶׁיֵּדְעוּ בּוֹ שְׁכֵנָיו.	Until one's neighbors become aware of it.
דִּבְרֵי רַבִּי מֵאִיר.	These are the words of Rabbi Meir.

b.

רַבִּי יְהוּדָה אוֹמֵר,	Rabbi Judah says:
שָׁלֹשׁ רְגָלִים,	"Until three festivals have passed
וְאַחַר הָרֶגֶל הָאַחֲרוֹן שִׁבְעָה יָמִים,	plus seven days after the third festival,
כְּדֵי	in order that the person who had lost the object
שֶׁיֵּלֵךְ לְבֵיתוֹ שְׁלֹשָׁה	might have three days to go home,
וְיַחֲזוֹר שְׁלֹשָׁה	three days to return,
וְיַכְרִיז יוֹם אֶחָד.	and one day to proclaim the loss."

---

1. Why does Rabbi Meir believe that a local announcement is sufficient? Why does Rabbi Judah maintain that a year-long national announcement is necessary? Which point of view do you prefer?

   _____
   _____

2. Why does Rabbi Judah allow time to return home after the third festival?

   _____
   _____

3. How long should one advertise the following finds today?

   A dog _____

   A wallet with $150.00 _____

   Diamond earrings worth $5,000 _____

   A sweater _____

   A tennis racket with initials on it _____

A Piece of Gemara

The Mishnah doesn't tell us whose opinion was to be followed, Rabbi Judah's or Rabbi Meir's. When we look at the Talmudic discussion of this Mishnaic passage (28b), we see how changing circumstances brought about new solutions.

> At first, in Temple times, anyone who found a lost object would announce his discovery in Jerusalem at each of the next three pilgrimage festivals and after that last pilgrimage festival, would continue making the announcement for seven more days...
>
> After the Temple was destroyed (and may it be rebuilt quickly and in our days), the rabbis changed the procedure and made it a practice for the finders of lost property to make announcements in local synagogues and houses of study since there was no longer any single place where all Jews gathered.
>
> Later, when a corrupt government came to power and the people were afraid that the government would take for itself any find of value, the sages changed the procedure again and made it a practice for a person to inform only one's immediate neighbors.

This piece of Gemara tells the story of how and why Jewish practice changed. Retell that story in your own words.

_____

_____

_____

_____

Then, based on this example, tell about one of the practices in a Mishnah which we have studied which should be changed to fit today's situation.

_____

_____

_____

_____

Sherry Advertises a Found Wallet...

Sherry was walking toward her car in the high school parking lot when she saw something on the ground. She picked it up. It was a brown leather wallet with five ten-dollar bills in it. The wallet contained no identification.

She put a notice on the school bulletin board saying: "If you lost a wallet with money in it, call Sherry, 555-3124."

Sherry received three calls. In each case, she asked the caller to describe the wallet and to tell how much money was in it. Max said that his wallet was black and that he had between fifty and a hundred dollars in it. Jill said that her lost wallet was red. It contained seven dollars. Roger said that he had lost a brown wallet with fifty dollars in it. Even though Roger correctly identified the color of the wallet and the amount of money in it, Sherry was suspicious of him. He had once been accused of stealing money from a student's locker and she knew for a fact that he had once cheated on an exam.

What should Sherry do with the wallet and the money?

_____
_____
_____

Bava Metzia, Chapter 2, Mishnah 7

a.

אָמַר אֶת־הָאֲבֵדָה	If a person says, "I have lost an object,"
וְלֹא אָמַר סִימָנֶיהָ,	but is unable to describe its identifying marks,
לֹא יִתֵּן לוֹ;	the finder should not give it to to that person;

b.

וְהָרַמַּאי	and if the claimant is known to be dishonest,
אַף עַל פִּי שֶׁאָמַר סִימָנֶיהָ,	even if the claimant can describe its identifying marks,
לֹא יִתֵּן לוֹ,	the finder should not give it to the claimant,
שֶׁנֶּאֱמַר,	for the Torah says that a find should remain with you,
עַד דְּרוֹשׁ אָחִיךָ אוֹתוֹ,	"UNTIL YOUR NEIGHBOR CLAIMS IT."
	This means that you should not give up the find
עַד שֶׁתִּדְרוֹשׁ אֶת־אָחִיךָ	until you investigate to determine
אִם רַמַּאי הוּא אִם אֵינוֹ רַמַּאי.	whether or not your "NEIGHBOR" is a deceiver.

---

1. What are the identifying marks of a wallet, a scarf, money, a camera, a soccer ball?
   _____
   _____

2. Are there circumstances under which you think that you should give up your find even when the claimant is unable to describe the identifying marks?
   _____
   _____

3. Are there times when you would turn over a find to someone whom you believe to be untrustworthy?
   _____
   _____

4. If Sherry is to follow the advice of the Mishnah, what should she do?
   _____
   _____

UNIT IX
Leila Cares for a Lost Cat...

Leila was driving home from work late at night when her headlights shone on a cat on the road. She put on the brakes and stopped just before hitting the stray animal. Leila got out of the car and took a look at the cat. She happened to be a cat lover and knew something about cats. She could tell immediately that this was a valuable Siamese cat, worth about $300.00. To remove it from further danger she put it into her car and took it home. She wanted to return it to its owner as soon as possible. She advertised her find in the paper. She bought equipment to care for the cat ($30.00). She took it to the vet ($35.00). She, of course, had to feed the cat ($10.00 per week). No one responded to her ad in the paper. She waited six weeks. Her total expenses by then had reached $125.00. She thought then that she should sell the cat and hold onto the $175.00 balance in case the owner appeared. Should she have waited six weeks? Should she have waited longer? What is your opinion?

Bava Metzia, Chapter 2, Mishnah 7

c.

כָּל־דָּבָר שֶׁעוֹשֶׂה וְאוֹכֵל   If someone finds an animal that works and eats,

יַעֲשֶׂה וְיֹאכַל,   then it must work and eat,

and the work that it performs will pay for the food that it eats;

d.

וְדָבָר שֶׁאֵין עוֹשֶׂה וְאוֹכֵל   But if someone finds an animal that eats but does not work,

יִמָּכֵר,   it should be sold.

שֶׁנֶּאֱמַר,   This is the reasoning. It says in the Torah,

וַהֲשֵׁבֹתוֹ לוֹ,   "YOU SHALL GIVE IT BACK,"

רְאֵה הֵיאַךְ   which means that you must take good care

תְּשִׁיבֶנּוּ לוֹ.   of the object you are returning.

---

1. Give several examples of animals which might earn their keep.

   _____

   _____

2. Give examples of animals whose food and care might cost the finder were he to keep them.

   _____

   _____

3. Why does the Mishnah require the finder to sell an unproductive animal? Why does the finder need to sell the animal in order to fulfill the injunction to take good care of the object he is returning?

   _____

   _____

4. How could the Mishnah help Leila decide about selling the cat?

   _____

Alex Needs to Sell An Earring He Found...

Alex's company was bought out by a large corporation. Many workers lost their jobs. Alex was laid off. Three months went by and he still couldn't find work. He was three months behind in his mortgage payments. If he didn't catch up by the end of the month, Alex's home would be foreclosed, and he, his wife, and three children would be evicted.

On the 23rd of the month, Alex found a diamond earring in the street worth $5,000.00. On the 25th of the month, he advertised his find in the paper. No one responded. Would it be right for Alex to sell the earring on the 30th in order to save his house?

_____

_____

The law in the State of Illinois (September 11, 1984) is that a find worth $100.00 or less becomes the property of the finder if the owner does not claim it within six months of the time that the advertisement appears. A find worth more than $100.00 becomes the finder's after a period of one year. Do you feel that this is a reasonable law? Would you amend it? How? How does the law in your state compare to the Illinois statute?

_____

_____

Bava Metzia, Chapter 2, Mishnah 7

e.

מַה־יְּהֵא בַדָּמִים?   **Q:** What should be done with the money obtained from the sale of a find?

f.

רַבִּי טַרְפוֹן אוֹמֵר, יִשְׁתַּמֵּשׁ בָּהֶן,   Rabbi Tarfon says: "One may use it, and therefore,
לְפִיכָךְ אִם אָבְדוּ חַיָּב בְּאַחֲרָיוּתָן.   if it is lost, one is responsible for it."

g.

רַבִּי עֲקִיבָא אוֹמֵר, לֹא יִשְׁתַּמֵּשׁ בָּהֶן,   Rabbi Akiba says: "One may not use it,
לְפִיכָךְ אִם אָבְדוּ אֵין חַיָּב בְּאַחֲרָיוּתָן.   and therefore, if it is lost, one is not responsible for it."

To understand the views of Rabbi Tarfon and Rabbi Akiba, we need to be familiar with part of a Mishnah which appears later in Bava Metzia (7:8). It explains that an unpaid guardian (who is not negligent) is not held liable for any loss that may occur to a guarded object, but that a borrower is liable in every case.

1. Why, according to Rabbi Tarfon, is the finder responsible if the money is lost?

2. Why, according to Rabbi Akiba, is the finder not liable if the money is lost?

3. Whose opinion do you favor, Rabbi Tarfon's or Rabbi Akiba's? Why?

4. Victor lost his Bulova watch. Marshall found it on the street. He put an ad in the paper and in the meantime wore the watch. When Victor called, Marshall had lost the watch. What is to be done?

5. Carol lost her puppy. Tomi found it and brought it home. The puppy got into the medicine cabinet and died from an overdose. Carol sued Tomi. Should Tomi have to pay?

UNIT X
Marjorie Saves an Orchid...

Visitors from all over the country came to the Flower and Plant Show where flowers and plants of all shapes and varieties were on display. When the show was over, Marjorie saw that someone had left a phaleonopsis orchid plant in the front lobby. The Convention Center was about to close. Marjorie knew that this fine orchid plant would never make it through the weekend in the lobby. It needed humidity and bright, indirect light. She took it home and gave it the required care. It took time and effort on her part to care for it, but she understood that the orchid plant was valuable. On Monday, she placed an ad in the paper announcing her find. When Marjorie told her friend Gayle what she had done, Gayle said that all that work was beyond the call of duty. She said that no one would expect a person to go to so much trouble to care for a lost object.

Under the circumstances, how would you best describe Marjorie's actions?

_____ required   _____ appropriate   _____ overdone

Explain your response.

_____
_____
_____

Bava Metzia, Mishnah 8

a.

מָצָא סְפָרִים	A person who finds scrolls
קוֹרֵא בָּהֶן אַחַת לִשְׁלֹשִׁים יוֹם,	should read them once in thirty days,
וְאִם אֵינוֹ יוֹדֵעַ לִקְרוֹת גּוֹלְלָן;	but if the finder doesn't know how to read, then they should be rolled.
אֲבָל לֹא יִלְמַד בָּהֶן בַּתְּחִלָּה,	However, a person should not study them for the first time,
וְלֹא יִקְרָא אַחֵר עִמּוֹ.	nor should they be read with someone else.

b.

מָצָא כְסוּת	A person who finds a garment
מְנַעֲרָהּ אַחַת לִשְׁלֹשִׁים יוֹם,	should take it out once in thirty days
וְשׁוֹטְחָהּ לְצָרְכָּהּ	and should spread it out for the benefit of the garment
אֲבָל לֹא לִכְבוֹדוֹ.	but not for one's own honor.

c.

כְּלֵי כֶסֶף וּכְלֵי נְחוֹשֶׁת	A person who finds vessels of silver or copper
מִשְׁתַּמֵּשׁ בָּהֶן לְצָרְכָּן	should use them for their benefit
אֲבָל לֹא לְשַׁחֲקָן.	but not to such an extent that they get worn out.
כְּלֵי זָהָב וּכְלֵי זְכוּכִית	A person who finds vessels of gold or glass
לֹא יִגַּע בָּהֶן עַד שֶׁיָּבֹא אֵלִיָּהוּ.	should not touch them until Elijah comes.

d.

מָצָא שַׂק אוֹ קוּפָּה	A person who finds a sack or a large basket
וְכָל דָּבָר שֶׁאֵין דַּרְכּוֹ לִטֹּל	or anything that one does not normally carry,
הֲרֵי זֶה לֹא יִטֹּל.	need not take it.

1. Why do scrolls need to be rolled once in thirty days? Can you think of something in our own day that is comparable?

2. Why does the Mishnah say that a person should not study them for the first time? Why should that person not read with someone else?

3. How does shaking or spreading out help the garment? Why does the Mishnah caution against spreading it out for one's honor?

4. Why are there different rules for silver and copper vessels on the one hand and for gold and glass vessels on the other?

5. Why is a finder not required to take home something that one normally doesn't carry? Do you agree? Explain.

6. Was caring for an orchid plant like rolling a scroll? If Marjorie wanted to follow the teachings of the Mishnah, did she have to bring the plant home and provide for its needs?

UNIT XI
Sheri Saves Fred Over and Over Again...

Fred is one of the people Sheri likes least of all. He always seems to be having a crisis of one sort or another. In Sheri's opinion, most of Fred's problems are of his own making.

At eight o'clock one evening Sheri gets a call from Fred. He is out of gas and needs help. This is the third time that Fred has run out of gas. Sheri is angry and refuses to help. What is your opinion of Sheri's refusal?

_____

_____

_____

_____

Bava Metzia, Chapter 2, Mishnah 9

a.

אֵיזוֹ הִיא אֲבֵדָה?	**Q:** What is considered a lost article?
מָצָא חֲמוֹר אוֹ פָרָה רוֹעִין בַּדֶּרֶךְ,	**A:** If someone finds a donkey or a cow grazing by the road,
אֵין זוֹ אֲבֵדָה;	it is not a lost article.
חֲמוֹר וְכֵלָיו הֲפוּכִין,	But if someone finds a donkey with its load overturned
פָרָה רָצָה בֵּין הַכְּרָמִים,	or a cow running in the vineyards,
הֲרֵי זוֹ אֲבֵדָה.	this should be considered a lost article.

b.

הֶחֱזִירָהּ וּבָרְחָה	If a finder returns it, and it runs away again,
הֶחֱזִירָהּ וּבָרְחָה,	and returns it again, and it runs away again,
אֲפִלּוּ אַרְבָּעָה וַחֲמִשָּׁה פְעָמִים	—even if this happens four or five times,
חַיָּב לְהַחֲזִירָהּ,	the finder is still required to return it,
שֶׁנֶּאֱמַר, הָשֵׁב תְּשִׁיבֵם.	for the Torah says, "YOU MUST BRING THEM BACK."

c.

הָיָה בָטֵל מִסֶּלַע	If a finder loses a sela (a coin) in wages
	by returning a lost object,
לֹא יֹאמַר לוֹ, תֶּן לִי סֶלַע,	the finder may not say to the owner, "Give me a sela."
אֶלָּא נוֹתֵן לוֹ שְׂכָרוֹ כְּפוֹעֵל בָּטֵל.	Rather, the owner pays the finder as an unemployed worker.
אִם יֵשׁ שָׁם בֵּית דִּין	If there is a *Bet Din* (a court) there,
	the finder may stipulate before the *Bet Din*
מַתְנֶה בִּפְנֵי בֵית דִּין;	to be reimbursed in full for the loss incurred in returning the lost object."
אִם אֵין שָׁם בֵּית דִּין בִּפְנֵי מִי יַתְנֶה,	If there is not a court there,
	before whom can the finder stipulate?
שֶׁלּוֹ קוֹדֵם.	In such a case, the finder's own interests take precedence.

1. Why does it make a difference whether or not the donkey's load is overturned? Why does it matter whether a cow is grazing on the road or running among the vineyards?

2. Do you agree that an article that is lost more than once still needs to be returned? Should there be some limit on the number of times a person should have to return the same object?

3. Why does the Mishnah not require the owner of a lost article to reimburse the finder for full lost wages? Why is only a court allowed to order such a payment? Do you agree?

4. Does the ruling of the Mishnah, "The finder's own interests take precedence," contradict the requirement, "YOU MUST BRING THEM BACK?" Explain.

5. What should you do if you see:
   a dog walking down the street? _____
   a dog digging up your flower bed? _____
   a cat on the street at night? _____
   a briefcase on a table in the library? _____
   a briefcase on a park bench? _____

6. Myra works at McDonald's for $6.00 an hour. One day Merle comes in for a hamburger and forgets her purse. Myra takes an hour and a half from work to return the purse and asks Merle to reimburse her for the $9.00 which she lost. Merle refuses. How would the Mishnah rule? What is your opinion?

7. Ted and Lil are driving to the Temple. Ted sees the Klein's dog which is lost and says that they should stop to return it. Lil says that they shouldn't do it because it will make them late for services. What is your opinion? Would your opinion be different if Ted were the rabbi of the congregation?

Bava Metzia, Chapter 2, Mishnah 10

a.

מְצָאָהּ בְּרֶפֶת	A person who finds an animal in a stable,
אֵין חַיָּב בָּהּ,	is not responsible for it,
בִּרְשׁוּת הָרַבִּים	but if one finds it on public property,
חַיָּב בָּהּ;	then it must be returned.

b.

	However, if he is a priest,
וְאִם הָיְתָה בְּבֵית הַקְּבָרוֹת	and the find is in a cemetery,
לֹא יִטַּמֵּא לָהּ.	he may not become defiled because of it.[1]

c.

אִם אָמַר לוֹ אָבִיו,	If his parent says to him,
הִטַּמֵּא,	"Become defiled because of it,"
אוֹ שֶׁאָמַר לוֹ,	or if his parent says to him,
אַל תַּחֲזִיר,	"Do not return it,"
לֹא יִשְׁמַע לוֹ.	he should not listen to the parent.

d.

פָּרַק	A person who unloads an animal that has fallen under its burden
וְטָעַן	and then loads it up again,
פָּרַק וְטָעַן,	unloads and loads,
אֲפִלּוּ אַרְבָּעָה וַחֲמִשָּׁה פְעָמִים,	even four or five times,
חַיָּב,	is still obligated to do it again,
שֶׁנֶּאֱמַר,	for it says in the Torah,
עָזֹב תַּעֲזֹב.	"YOU MUST RAISE IT."[2]
הָלַךְ וְיָשַׁב לוֹ וְאָמַר,	If the owner walks away and sits down and says,
הוֹאִיל וְעָלֶיךָ מִצְוָה,	"Since the mitzvah is incumbent upon you,
אִם רְצוֹנְךָ לִפְרוֹק פְּרוֹק,	if you want to unload, unload,"
פָּטוּר,	then the finder is exempt,
שֶׁנֶּאֱמַר, עִמּוֹ.	for the Torah says, "YOU **MUST** RAISE IT WITH THE OWNER."[3]

אִם הָיָה זָקֵן אוֹ חוֹלֶה	But if the owner is old or sick,
חַיָּב.	then that person is obligated to unload
	even without the owner's participation.

e.

מִצְוָה מִן הַתּוֹרָה לִפְרוֹק אֲבָל לֹא לִטְעוֹן,	The mitzvah from the Torah is to unload but not to load,
רַבִּי שִׁמְעוֹן אוֹמֵר,	but Rabbi Simeon says,
אַף לִטְעוֹן.	"One must also assist in loading."
רַבִּי יוֹסֵי הַגְּלִילִי אוֹמֵר,	Rabbi Yosi the Galilean says,
אִם הָיָה עָלָיו יֶתֶר עַל מַשָּׂאוֹ	"If the animal had more than a proper load,
אֵין זָקוּק לוֹ,	one is not required to help the owner,
שֶׁנֶּאֱמַר, תַּחַת מַשָּׂאוֹ,	for the Torah says 'UNDER **ITS** LOAD,'
מַשּׂאוּי שֶׁיָּכוֹל לַעֲמוֹד בּוֹ.	which means a burden which it can bear."

[1] This refers to Leviticus 21:1: ADONAI SAID TO MOSES, "SPEAK TO THE KOHANIM, THE SONS OF AARON, AND SAY TO THEM: 'YOU SHALL NOT MAKE YOURSELVES IMPURE THROUGH CONTACT WITH THE DEAD.'"

[2] This is a reference to Exodus 23:5, "IF YOU SEE THE ASS OF A PERSON WHOM YOU HATE PROSTRATE UNDER ITS LOAD, AND WOULD AVOID RAISING IT, YOU MUST RAISE IT WITH THE OWNER." The use of an intensive form of the verb "RAISE" suggests to the author of the Mishnah that the animal must be raised many times, if necessary.

[3] The Mishnah takes the words "WITH THE OWNER" to mean that one is required to raise the animal only if the owner of the animal also helps in the task.

1. Why does the Mishnah say that an animal found on public property should be returned to its owner? Isn't it possible that the owner left the animal in a public place and is planning to return for it?

2. According to the Mishnah, what should Sheri have done when Fred ran out of class for the third time?

3. Barbara finds four tickets for tomorrow's Chicago Bears football game in a wallet. The name and address are in the wallet, but the phone number is unlisted. Barbara wants to return the wallet, but the address is in a bad neighborhood and her father says she shouldn't go there. If she wants to follow the Mishnah, what should she do? What is your opinion?

4. Why does the Mishnah get off the subject of lost and found and begin dealing with the subject of loading and unloading?

UNIT XII
Bava Metzia, Chapter 2, Mishnah 11

אֲבֵדָתוֹ	If someone's lost article
וַאֲבֵדַת אָבִיו,	and one's parent's lost article need attention,
אֲבֵדָתוֹ קוֹדֶמֶת;	one's own takes precedence.
אֲבֵדָתוֹ	Between one's own lost article
וַאֲבֵדַת רַבּוֹ,	and one's teacher's lost article,
שֶׁלּוֹ קוֹדֶמֶת;	one's own takes precedence.
אֲבֵדַת אָבִיו	Between one's parent's lost article
וַאֲבֵדַת רַבּוֹ,	and one's teacher's lost article,
שֶׁל רַבּוֹ קוֹדֶמֶת,	one's teacher's takes precedence,
שֶׁאָבִיו הֱבִיאוֹ לָעוֹלָם הַזֶּה,	for one's parent brought one into this world,
וְרַבּוֹ שֶׁלִּמְּדוֹ חָכְמָה	but one's teacher, who taught one wisdom,
מְבִיאוֹ לְחַיֵּי הָעוֹלָם הַבָּא;	brings one into life of the world to come.
וְאִם אָבִיו חָכָם (שָׁקוּל כְּנֶגֶד רַבּוֹ)	But if one's parent is a scholar,
שֶׁל אָבִיו קוֹדֶמֶת.	then one's parent's takes precedence.
הָיָה אָבִיו וְרַבּוֹ נוֹשְׂאִין מַשָּׂאוּי,	If one's parent and one's teacher were each carrying a burden,
מַנִּיחַ אֶת-שֶׁל רַבּוֹ	one must first relieve one's teacher of a burden
וְאַחַר כָּךְ מַנִּיחַ אֶת-שֶׁל אָבִיו.	and then relieve one's parent.
הָיָה אָבִיו וְרַבּוֹ בְּבֵית הַשֶּׁבִי,	If one's parent and one's teacher were in captivity,
פּוֹדֶה אֶת-רַבּוֹ	one must first ransom one's teacher
וְאַחַר כָּךְ פּוֹדֶה אֶת-אָבִיו;	and then ransom one's parent.
וְאִם הָיָה אָבִיו חָכָם,	But if one's parent was a scholar,
פּוֹדֶה אֶת-אָבִיו	then one must first ransom one's parent
וְאַחַר כָּךְ פּוֹדֶה אֶת-רַבּוֹ.	and then ransom one's teacher.

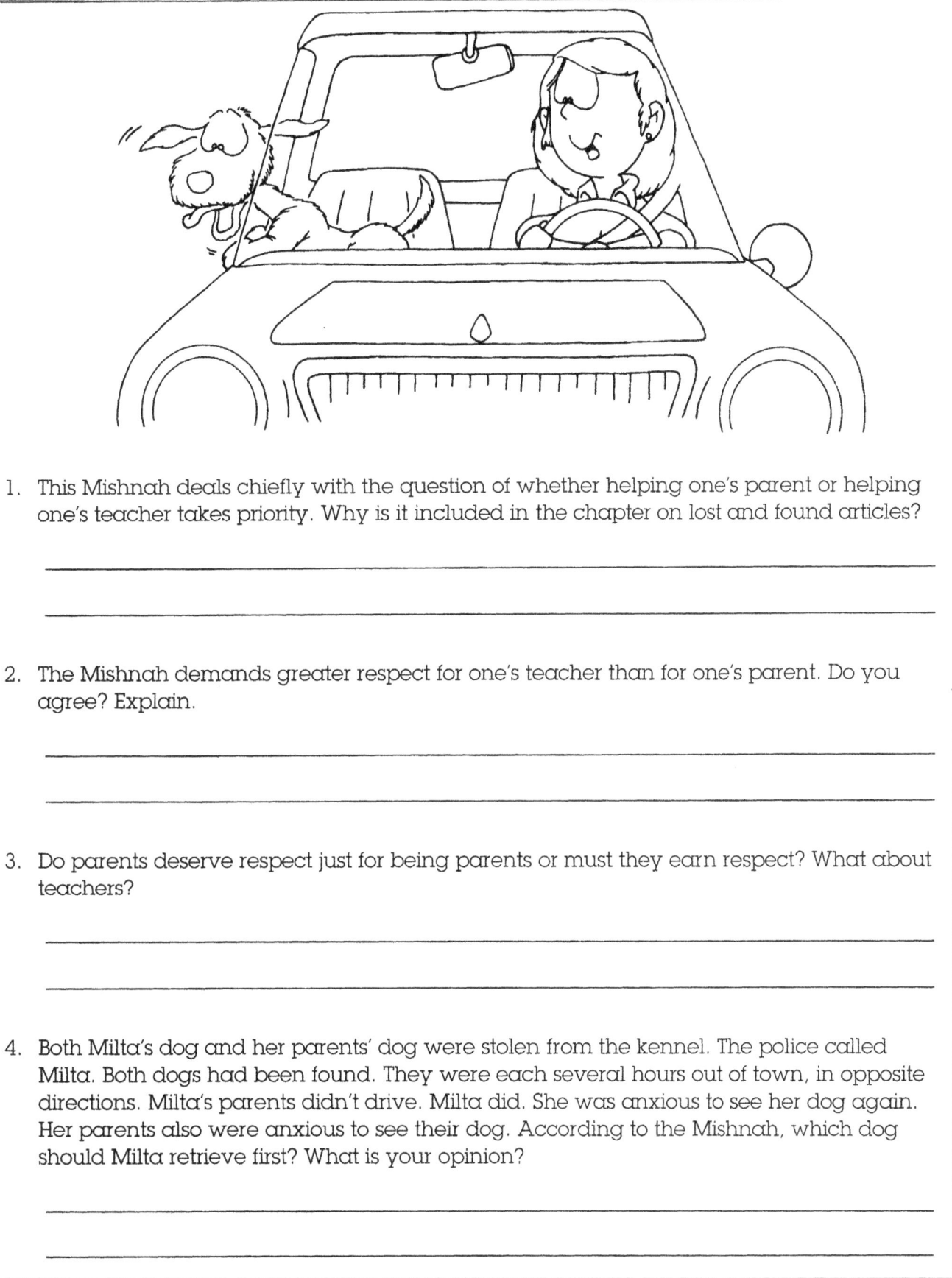

1. This Mishnah deals chiefly with the question of whether helping one's parent or helping one's teacher takes priority. Why is it included in the chapter on lost and found articles?

   _____

   _____

2. The Mishnah demands greater respect for one's teacher than for one's parent. Do you agree? Explain.

   _____

   _____

3. Do parents deserve respect just for being parents or must they earn respect? What about teachers?

   _____

   _____

4. Both Milta's dog and her parents' dog were stolen from the kennel. The police called Milta. Both dogs had been found. They were each several hours out of town, in opposite directions. Milta's parents didn't drive. Milta did. She was anxious to see her dog again. Her parents also were anxious to see their dog. According to the Mishnah, which dog should Milta retrieve first? What is your opinion?

   _____

   _____

REVIEW

What Do You Do?

1. You find three ten-dollar bills in the synagogue parking lot.

2. You find a diamond ring in the street.

3. You find a five-dollar bill on the sidewalk.

4. You find a twenty-dollar bill on your neighbor's front lawn.

5. Your friend leaves her tennis racquet in front of your house. You keep it for her but decide to use it once. In the middle of the game, a string breaks.

Match a Mishnah

Using the list at the bottom of the page, show which Mishnah teaches each of the following principles:

_____ 1. People can have equal claims to the same object.

_____ 2. There are times when a person should disregard the words of a parent.

_____ 3. One should be patient with people who make a habit of losing things.

_____ 4. A person should honor a teacher even more than a parent.

_____ 5. A finder may keep something that cannot be identified.

_____ 6. One is not required to incur personal loss in order to return a lost item.

_____ 7. The owner of a private home owns whatever is found within it.

_____ 8. While waiting for someone to claim a find, a person should guard it carefully.

_____ 9. A person must try to discover the owner of a find that can be identified.

_____ 10. If the money from the sale of a found animal is lost, the finder is liable.

A. "Even... four or five times, the finder is still required to return it." (2:9)

B. "You must take good care of the object you are returning." (2:7)

C. "If someone finds something... on the inside, it belongs to the owner of the house". (2:3)

D. "Between one's parent's lost article and one's teacher's lost article, one's teacher's takes precedence." (2:11)

E. "Scattered money ... belongs to the finder." (2:1)

F. "One may use it, and therefore, if it is lost, one is responsible for it." (2:7)

G. "They should divide it." (1:1)

H. "Any lost object which has identifying signs ... must be proclaimed." (2:5)

I. "The finder's own interests take precedence." (2:9)

J. "If his parent says... 'Do not return it,' he should not listen to the parent." (2:10)

The class is divided into pairs. Each pair is assigned one of the above ten principles taught in the Mishnah and dramatizes a situation in which the principle can be applied. The students discuss each dramatization.

Choose a Mishnah

Look back over the Mishnayot that we have read. Which Mishnah do you consider to be the most important one of all, or the one that could have the greatest influence on your life if you remember to follow it? First copy the Mishnah (or the part of the Mishnah) which you have chosen. Then explain the reason for your selection.

_____

_____

_____

_____

Returning to Judith

This book began with a story about Judith, who found a gold necklace on a bus. Reread the story. Tell what you think Judith should do. Is your view the same now as it was before you began your study of these two chapters of Mishnah? Explain.

_____

_____

_____

Summing Up

What is the overriding principle taught in the first two chapters of Bava Metzia? How can this principle be applied in our own day beyond the subject of lost and found?

_____

_____

_____

_____